BY-LAWS AND JOB DESCRIPTIONS FOR THE
FOR THE
ECCLESIASTICAL JURISDICTION

I0412805

A MODEL FOR JURISDICTIONAL ADMINISTRATION AND OPERATION

Fourth Edition

Malcolm W. Coby, Ph. D.

BYLAWS AND JOB DESCRIPTIONS FOR THE JURISDICTION

Table of Contents

ACKNOWLEDGMENTS

The original committee on Job Descriptions for the Oklahoma Southeast Jurisdiction of the Church of God in Christ, Inc. met on January 4, 1988 at the Victory Temple Church of God in Christ. The following persons were members of this committee: Elder Malcolm W. Coby, Ph. D. (Secretary-author), Elder Mark C. B. Hannah, Jr., D.D., Elder Clyde McFadden, Jr., Elder James W. Powell, Jr., Elder Landis Powell, D.Ph., Elder Otis D. Thompson (Chair), and Superintendent Bobby L. Williams, D.D.

In 1992, Dr. Malcolm Coby, at the request of Bishop Lawson, wrote and submitted a proposal for Bylaws of the Jurisdiction. These bylaws were adopted in the Jurisdictional assembly and are incorporated in this document.

INTRODUCTION

This fourth edition was inspired by the author's original work submitted to the Oklahoma committee. The current work is presented as a model to my colleagues in the Board of Bishops. It is not presumed to be a definitive work, but a work in progress. It presents ideas toward identifying the roles and responsibilities of personnel to function at the jurisdictional level of church ministry and administration.

Obviously, these descriptions only represent current ideologies and may be adjusted by the Jurisdictional Bishop at his discretion. Therefore, for each personnel identified, the term of office shall run concurrently with that of the Bishop. However, the Bishop shall have the power to remove such officers at his discretion.

This twenty-first century generates a number of questions about the future of our church as well as the world in which we live. The five thousand need to be fed again, but will we have the loaves prepared for the dinner? Deliverance is still needed for those addicted to drugs, alcohol, and sin in any form, but will the church have the power to bring forth new souls into the kingdom? This administration prayerfully submits its talents and resources to the resolution of these and other issues in America and the world.

This "manual of operation", entitled Bylaws and Job Descriptions for the Ecclesiastical Jurisdiction, constitutes the guidebook developed for the Oklahoma Southeast Ecclesiastical Jurisdiction. Ministry cannot be effective unless it is organized and Spirit-led. This is writer is thoroughly convinced that this generation of godly leaders has a mandate from the Council of Heaven to identify and implement a structure of ecclesiastical duties that will effectively serve this generation. As the men of Isachaar, we must be people and leaders who are cognizant of the times and what Israel (the church) ought to do.

This author recognizes that the need to supplement the job descriptions as well as amend the bylaws will always exist. However, it is our hope that, at this juncture, an identifiable direction and structure will provide motivation for all concerned and involved to give the best of their service.

Therefore, it is not the intention of this publication to produce a structure of governance that only reflects current personnel and or practices. On the contrary, it is more important to develop a document with which future administrations can build upon. As Jurisdictional Prelate, it is my desire for this document to serve as an instrument of value for many years to come. Also, please note that these bylaws are based on the Constitution of the Church of God in Christ, Inc., with worldwide headquarters in Memphis, Tennessee. This document does not replace or conflict with our international constitution. Sincere appreciation is extended to all who contributed to this endeavor. This document does not replace or conflict with our international constitution. Sincere appreciation is extended to all who contributed to this endeavor.

BY-LAWS OF THE

ECCLESIASTICAL JURISDICTION

PREAMBLE:

We the members, pastors, and officers of the Church of God in Christ, {Name of Your Jurisdiction} in order to respond to the great commission of Matthew 28:19, i.e. "Go ye therefore, and teach all nations; do hereby affirm and declare our unwavering faith in our Creator and in Jesus Christ His only begotten Son. It is with this focus that we hereby establish these Byelaws for operation.

We hereby declare our loyalty to the President of the United States of America and to the Constitution of this country. We further pledge our allegiance and fidelity to the flag, and to the republic for which it stands. Nevertheless, as God-loving, peaceful, and law-abiding people, we claim our heritage and natural right to worship God according to the dictates of our own conscience. We therefore abstain from war in all of its forms in accordance with our belief that the shedding of human blood is contrary to the teachings of our Lord and Saviour Jesus Christ. Furthermore, we adhere to the resolution of all national and international disputes in a peaceful manner.

Additionally, in accordance with the Constitution and charter of the Church of God in Christ, Incorporated, with international headquarters in Memphis, Tennessee, we the members, pastors, and officers of the Church of God in Christ, {Name of Your Jurisdiction} Inc., do hereby formulate these Bylaws in full compliance with said Constitution of the national church. These Bylaws shall not in any way be construed to be in conflict with said national church, nor its constitution or charter.

Finally, it is with grateful appreciation and in loving memory of our founding fathers that we prayerfully dedicate the establishment of these Bylaws to the memory of our revered founder Bishop Charles Harrison Mason and the former prelates of this Jurisdiction who now rest in the presence of Jesus Christ, namely, Bishop E.L. Thompson, Bishop Coy Brown, Bishop W. E. Jefferies, and Bishop F. D. Lawson, Jr. We are grateful for the legacy they left with us.

ARTICLE I: NAME

The name of this organization shall be {Name of Your Jurisdiction} Church of God in Christ, Inc., with corporate office in the city of {Name of Your City} {Name of Your County or Parish} County, in the Jurisdictional of {Name of Your Jurisdiction}, and conducting its business throughout the {Name of Your Jurisdiction}.

ARTICLE II: PURPOSE:

The primary purpose of this organization (corporation) shall be as follows:

To cultivate, promote, promulgate, and extend the teachings, precepts, practices, and discipline of the Church of God in Christ denomination, and to conduct and maintain a Christian organization of churches in accordance with said principles, creed, precepts, practices, and discipline of said denomination throughout the Jurisdictional of {Name of Your Jurisdiction} as presently or henceforth directed by the national church.

The above requirement shall not be deemed to preclude a statement of general purpose or power, or to restrict the right of the corporation to engage in other legal activity, to wit: To purchase, receive, take, acquire, hold, sell, convey, or otherwise dispose of property, whether it be real, personal, or mixed; To receive property by devise or bequest; subject to the laws regulating the transfer of property, real or personal, including shares of stocks, bonds, and securities of other corporations, to wit: Said property is to be held in trust for the use and benefit of the members, pastors, and officers of the Church of God in Christ, {Name of Your Jurisdiction} with national headquarters in the City of Memphis, Shelby County, Tennessee, and subject to the charter, constitution, laws, and doctrines of said church, now in full force and effect, or as they may be hereafter amended, changed, or modified by the General Assembly of said church;

1. To act as trustees under any condition incidental to the principal subject of the corporation, and to receive, hold, administer, and extend the funds of property subject to such trust; To convey, exchange, lease, mortgage, encumber, transfer upon trust, or otherwise dispose of all property, real or personal, or mixed;

2. To borrow money, contract debts, and issue bonds, notes, debentures, and secure the same; but shall not have the authority to issue capital stock;

3. To contract and be contracted with; To do all acts necessary or expedient for the administration of the affairs and attainment of the purpose of the corporation; The purpose of this corporation neither includes nor contemplates pecuniary gain or profit from or for the members thereof.

ARTICLE III: MEMBERSHIP

The membership of the corporation of the Church of God in Christ, {Name of Your Jurisdiction} Inc., shall consist of the local churches and their members, pastors, and officers who voluntarily associate themselves with said corporation. No local church or its members shall have full status in the Jurisdiction until it has been registered by the Jurisdictional Bishop in the office of the General Secretary of the national church, who shall then issue to the Jurisdictional Bishop a certificate of membership for the local church.

Section 1. Neither a local church, whose Jurisdictional Bishop has not received a Certificate of Membership from the national office in Memphis, Tennessee, nor any member thereof, shall be entitled to enjoy the rights and privileges of membership in the Church of God in Christ, in general, or the Corporation of the {Name of Your Jurisdiction} Church of God in Christ, in particular.

Section 2. A local church which has been accepted by the {Name of Your Jurisdiction} of the Church of God in Christ and issued a Certificate of Membership shall not withdraw or sever its relations with said Jurisdiction except by and with the permission of the Jurisdictional Bishop and the Jurisdictional Assembly; and furthermore, upon withdrawal, shall cease and desist from using the name "Church of God in Christ", until and if it duly becomes restored in said Jurisdiction.

Section 3. All rules of operation of local churches shall be established and governed by the National Constitution and Charter of the Church of God in Christ, Incorporated including all future amendments; this shall include but not be limited to the following: Selection of trustees, use or sale of real estate and other church property, church membership, rules of transfer of membership, etc.

Section 4. There are no classes of members in the corporation and people of all colors, races or nationalities are eligible for membership.

ARTICLE IV: STRUCTURE OF THE CHURCH

Section 1. The Jurisdictional Bishop shall be the spiritual leader and chief administrative officer of the Corporation. In civil terms, he is the President of the corporate body. He shall have the final authority in deciding all matters pertaining to the spiritual and business affairs of the Corporation. As President, he shall sign all certificates, contracts, deeds, and other instruments of the Corporation. All decisions of the Boards, Trustees, Department Heads, and other officers shall be subject to the authorization of the President. The President's decisions and authority shall therefore be final.

Section 2. The Constitution of the Church of God in Christ does not provide for a vice president at the Jurisdictional level. However, the Jurisdictional Bishop may designate someone to represent him in his absence at his pleasure.

Section 3. The Secretary of the Jurisdiction (Corporation) shall be appointed by the President (Bishop) and shall keep the minutes of all meetings; shall have charge of the seal and the corporate books and shall make such reports and perform such duties as are required of him/her by the Corporation, and shall also sign all certificates, contracts, deeds, and other instruments of the Corporation. The Assistant Secretary shall perform the duties of the secretary in his/her absence or disability or as otherwise directed by the Corporation.

Section 4. The Treasurer shall have custody of all monies and securities of the Corporation and shall keep regular books of account. He/She shall disburse the funds of the Corporation or as may be required of him/her, shall make an accounting of all his/her transactions as Treasurer and of the financial condition of the Corporation.

Section 5. Other members of the corporate structure shall consist of: Trustee Board, Jurisdictional Assembly, Superintendent's Council, Elder's Council, Department of Women, Department Heads, Local Churches, and other officers and officials as the Corporation shall deem necessary.

ARTICLE V: DUTIES OF THE BOARD OF TRUSTEES

Section 1. The property and business affairs of the Corporation shall be exercised and conducted by the Board of Trustees, consisting of no less than seven (7) and no more than eleven (11) members to be recommended by the members of the Jurisdictional Assembly by secret ballot and approved by the Bishop at the annual meeting every four (4) years and shall be relieved from duty for cause by the Jurisdictional Bishop. Such removal shall be in accordance with guidelines specified in the National Constitution of the Church of God in Christ, Inc.

Section 2. The Bishop shall be an ex officio member of the Board of Trustees and entitled to vote.

Section 3. In case of a vacancy on the Board of Trustees, the remaining Trustees shall submit to the Bishop for his approval, the name of some person to fill out the unexpired term until the next annual meeting.

Section 4. The majority of the Board of Trustees shall constitute a quorum for the transaction of business.

ARTICLE VI: THE JURISDICTIONAL ASSEMBLY

The Jurisdictional Assembly consists of the bodies of the Church of God in Christ composed of the following members, in accordance with the rules and regulations of the national church to wit:

1. Jurisdictional Bishop;

2. Supervisor of the Department of Women's Department;

3. All Pastors of Local Churches;

4. Ordained Elders;

5. District Missionaries;

6. Jurisdictional Department Heads;

7. Six (6) Lay Delegate from Each Jurisdictional District.

ARTICLE VII: MEETINGS

Regular business meetings of the Corporation shall be held in April, July, and December of each year. The December meeting shall be considered the annual meeting. Two-thirds of the delegates registered shall constitute a quorum for conducting business.

ARTICLE VIII: AMENDMENTS

These Bylaws may be amended by a majority vote of delegates present in the Jurisdictional Assembly with the approval of the Bishop.

Section 1: Job Descriptions

The Jurisdictional Job Descriptions below are hereby adopted and considered part of the Bylaws that govern the Southeast Jurisdiction of {Name of Your Jurisdiction} Churches of God in Christ, Inc. Certain job descriptions such as pastor, elder, and missionary are purposely not included. They are fully described in the Official Manual of the Church of God in Christ. This document supplements said manual by including job descriptions not fully described therein.

JURISDICTIONAL SECRETARY

The Jurisdictional Secretary is appointed by the Jurisdictional Bishop to handle general correspondence from the General Secretary. This description requires a person who will preserve excellence in record keeping and other duties as identified.

General Duties:

1. Manage the clerical responsibilities of the Jurisdiction.
   a. Keeping track of information
   b. Storing and cataloging new information and documents

2. Manage all communications for the Jurisdiction.
   a. Storing communications in retrievable files
   b. Receive correspondence and file appropriately

3. Develop and maintain a records retrieval system.

4. Receive and submit all correspondence requested by the General Secretary's office.

5. Supervise and manage other persons on this staff.

Specific Responsibilities

2. Maintain an updated roster of the clergy, churches and Women's Department workers.
   a. Conduct an annual update campaign

b. Solicit information via Superintendents and Department Heads

3. Register and certify all delegates to and national meetings.
   a. Conduct annual certification campaign
   b. Submit appropriate certification forms to the General Secretary and store copies of the same in the jurisdictional files.

4. Write official letters for the Bishop and Jurisdictional officers which includes but is not limited to the following:
   a. Letters to the national church or other jurisdictional Bishops
   b. Letters of condolence and resolution to the following:
      i. The demise of other Bishops and or their wives
      ii. The demise of jurisdictional pastors, missionaries or their spouses
      iii. The demise of close relatives of jurisdictional members

5. Record minutes of Jurisdictional Assembly meetings.

a. Store the minutes in a retrievable system
b. Send minutes of previous meeting to jurisdictional leaders and pastors

5. Record documents of appointments, decisions, etc.
    a. Store said appointments in a data base
    b. Review appointments annually for vacancies

EXECUTIVE SECRETARY

The executive secretary is appointed by the Jurisdictional Bishop to assist him in personal communications, appointment scheduling, travel arrangements, etc. as determined by the Jurisdictional Bishop.

General Duties

1. Prepare and send all personal correspondence of the Bishop.

2. Manage telephone communications for the Bishop.

3. Maintain the Bishop's itinerary and communicate to him the same.

Specific Responsibilities

1. Set up conference calls for the Bishop when designated.

2. Write personal letters and memos for the Bishop.

3. Keep files of all incoming and outgoing correspondence.

4. Screen incoming calls and informs the Bishop.

5. Keep a record of all long distance and other toll calls.

6. Upon approval of the Bishop, defer calls to other department heads when appropriate.

7. Assist the Bishop in typing sermons or speeches.

8. Keep the Bishop's resume updated with a recent photograph (every three to five years).

9. Keep a current itinerary of the Bishop's appointments.

10. Keep the Bishop reminded by call, in person, or by written communication of his schedule.

ADMINISTRATIVE ASSISTANTS

The purpose of this section is to describe a workable job description for administrative assistants. These are roles that must clearly identify duties that do not conflict with other jurisdictional officers. These are also roles that must neither diminish nor interfere with the duties of the jurisdictional bishop. The job descriptions that follow will model formats that are without and with numerical designation. In other words, it is the discretion of the Bishop to either name functions of administrative assistants without making first, second or third distinctions or to name assistants with numerical distinctions.

The role of the administrative assistant is that of a servant. He is a member of the executive cabinet of the jurisdictional bishop. He is hand picked by the bishop to serve at his pleasure while he is in office. Therefore, the primary role of the administrative assistant is to assist or support the bishop in the discharge of his duties as that assistant is assigned. He is neither the junior bishop nor the assistant bishop. He is only an assistant to the bishop for purposes of effective administration.

The administrative assistant will hold office during a term concurrent with that of the jurisdictional bishop. His tenure, therefore, may end at any time at the discretion of the bishop with or without cause. His term automatically ends with the demise or termination of the bishop who appointed him.

ADMINISTRATIVE ASSISTANTS
WITHOUT NUMERICAL DISTINCTION

General Duties:

1. Support the Vision and Direction of the Jurisdictional Bishop.

2. Represent the Bishop at his discretion and direction.

3. He shall be an ordained elder in good standing.

Specific Duties:

It is the prerogative of the Jurisdictional Bishop to appoint any assistant to any of the duties (Commissioners) that follow. The following offices are suggestions for the Jurisdictional Bishop to utilize.

COMMISSIONER OF FACILITIES

1. Provide supervision of repair and maintenance of the interior and the exterior of the Jurisdictional headquarters facility.

2. Identify necessary repairs and or maintenance needs.

3. Obtain approval for repairs and or maintenance prior to their completion.

4. Utilizing the established fiscal procedures, secure necessary funds and or resources for approved repairs or maintenance needs.

5. Serve as the contact person for contractors and oversee their successful completion of any contractual agreements prior to paying for them.

COMMISSIONER FOR JURISDICTIONAL COMMUNITY MATTERS

1. Communicate with city and Jurisdictional government officials on matters affecting, or with the potential to affect, the jurisdictional organization.

2. Keep the Bishop and the jurisdiction apprised of governmental plans.

3. Serve as a direct liaison between the Bishop and the various departments of the Jurisdiction.

4. Assist the Bishop as directed in matters of business, such as document reviews and brings matters of concern to his attention.

5. Work in cooperation with the office of the Jurisdictional Secretary to secure an ad for the national Holy Convocation in Memphis, Tennessee or other national meetings as directed by the Jurisdictional Bishop.

COMMISSIONER OF FINANCE

1. Supervise the collection of Jurisdictional finances during Jurisdictional meetings.

2. Supervise the collection of all Jurisdictional finances including, but not limited to Jurisdictional and national reports, building fund money, etc.

   a. This includes the organization of a Jurisdictional finance system, and office staff to properly fulfil the office of Commissioner of Finance.

   b. This includes coordinating information related to finances between his office and the Jurisdictional Secretary's Office.

3. Assist the Bishop in the collection of Jurisdictional revenue representing him in various locations in the Jurisdiction as he designates.

4. Supervise the operation of concession stands and the manager of concessions.

5. Attend and participate in all meetings of the Trustee Board

6. The Commissioner of Finance is not an elected member of the Trustee Board, but is appointed by the Jurisdictional Bishop and shall serve tenure on said board at the pleasure of the Jurisdictional Bishop.

7. He shall analyze and advise the Trustees' use of budgetary guidelines.

8. He shall approve and monitor Trustee fund raising projects.

9. He shall monitor and advise the Trustee Board in actions related to the tentative purchase, sale, or exchange of church owned or church related properties.

10. Provide leadership in the development of the budget.

11. 11 Approve the actions of the Trustee Board in the absence of the Bishop; however, such decisions shall lend themselves to adjustment by the Bishop.

COMMISSIONER OF CONVENTIONS

1. Chair the program committee for the two Jurisdictional conventions.

2. Supervise the preparation of programs for the Jurisdictional meetings.

3. As chair of the Program Committee, submit the program outline to the Bishop for his approval at least 60 days in advance of the April Ministers' and Workers' Meeting, and no later than 30 days prior to the July Holy Convocation.

4. Serve as Chairman of A.I.M (Auxiliaries in Ministry).

5. Chair any subsequent reorganization of A.I.M and report such reorganization to the Bishop and Jurisdictional Assembly for final approval.

6. Serve as liaison between the A. I. M. Presidents and the Executive Board.

7. Meet with the Women's Department to identify the type of role the Bishop and clergy of the Jurisdiction will perform in the Jurisdictional Women's Convention.

COMMISSIONER OF EDUCATION

General Duties:

1. Supervise the operation of the Board of Education

2. He shall monitor disbursement of funds for said board

3. Provide leadership in overall educational programming.

a. Provide specific leadership in the development of programs of education during the Jurisdictional meetings and at other times at the pleasure of the Bishop.

b. Arrange and conduct seminar training in the Convocation and Minister's and Worker's Meeting.

4. Supervise the operation of educational ministries of the Jurisdiction such as Bible colleges and Christian schools.

5. Assist the Bishop in arrangements for and the conducting of an annual leadership workshop or retreat.

6. Develop ways of supporting education of our youth.

Specific Responsibilities:

1. Arrange and conduct an annual Leadership Workshop or Retreat for all Jurisdictional officers, department heads, and/or pastors.

2. Develop a means of generating scholarships for graduating seniors at the Jurisdictional level.

3. Identify topics and personnel for Convocation and April meeting seminars.

4. Schedule the above with the Commissioner of Conventions.

5. Submit to the Bishop the content and format for the leadership retreat or workshop.

6. Oversee the development and operation of the Charles Harrison Mason System of Bible Colleges of {Name of Your Jurisdiction}, and other such programs of education as shall be developed.

7. Chair the investigation of legal issues related to Jurisdictional business, following the guidelines as set forth in the Official Manual of the Church of God in Christ.

8. Chair the Jurisdictional Assemblies

ADMINISTRATIVE ASSISTANTS

WITH NUMERICAL DISTINCTION

PURPOSE

The purpose of this section is to provide a workable job description for designated administrative assistants in the jurisdiction. These are roles that must clearly delineate duties that do not conflict with other jurisdictional officers. It is also a role that must not diminish nor interfere with the duties of the jurisdictional Bishop. The job descriptions that follow will provide numerical designations. However, these designations are only for purposes of identification. They may be reassigned at any time by the jurisdictional bishop.

DEFINITION

The role of the administrative assistant is that of a servant. He is a member of the executive cabinet of the jurisdictional bishop. He is hand picked by the bishop to serve at his pleasure while he is in office. Therefore, the primary role of the administrative assistant is to assist or support the bishop in the discharge of his duties as that assistant is assigned. He is neither the junior bishop nor the assistant bishop. He is only an assistant to the bishop for purposes of effective administration.

TERM OF OFFICE

The administrative assistant will hold office during a term concurrent with that of the jurisdictional bishop unless removed. His tenure, therefore, may end at any time at the discretion of the Bishop with or without cause. His term automatically ends with the death or termination of the bishop who appointed him.

FIRST ADMINISTRATIVE ASSISTANT

QUALIFICATIONS   The first administrative assistant shall have served as a successful pastor or superintendent for at least ten years. His success as pastor shall include proven church growth, sound business administration, and the ability to lead other leaders. It is also important that this assistant have formal administrative experience and or training in the same. This shall include but not be limited to college level courses in administration, certificates from administration seminars, or secular job experience in administration. He must have the ability to delegate authority and respond to superiors. Finally, he must have a sound history of support to the jurisdiction. In other words, he must be consistent in Jurisdictional and national reports as well as a tither to the jurisdiction.

DUTIES

The primary duty of the first administrative assistant is to provide assistance to the bishop in the coordination of administrative services. He is to assist in the collection of Jurisdictional and national reports. He will work in concert with the commissioner of finance and the jurisdictional secretary in this matter. His particular role is that of the organization and monitoring of the reporting procedure. This includes the use of an up to date data retrieval system and to provide leadership in developing strategies for improvement of said system.

The first administrative assistant is to also provide leadership on behalf of the bishop in the development of the Jurisdictional budget. Again, working in cooperation with the commissioner of finance office, he is to provide proper input in the development of the budget after careful consultation with the jurisdictional bishop. He is the Bishop's representative in this matter.

It is also the responsibility of the first administrative assistant to communicate with public officials in civic matters that affect or have the potential to affect the constituency of the jurisdiction. In this role, he functions as a liaison for the jurisdiction. He may also represent the Bishop, as the Bishop desires.

SECOND ADMINISTRATIVE ASSISTANT

QUALIFICATIONS

The second administrative assistant shall also have served as a successful pastor or superintendent for at least ten years. His success as pastor shall include proven church growth, sound business administration, and the ability to lead other leaders. It is also important that this assistant have formal administrative experience and or training in the same. This shall include but not be limited to college level courses in administration, certificates from administration seminars, or secular job experience in administration. The second administrative assistant must have the ability to delegate authority and respond to his superior appropriately.

Finally, he must have a sound history of support to the jurisdiction. In other words, he must be consistent in Jurisdictional and national reports as well as a tither to the jurisdiction.

DUTIES

The second administrative assistant has the responsibility of assisting the Bishop in the coordination of jurisdictional operations. In brief, he is the Chief Officer of Operations for the Jurisdiction In this capacity; he shall be responsible for the supervision of maintenance and development of the jurisdictional headquarters. This includes but is not limited to the selection of personnel for maintenance and upkeep of the jurisdictional headquarters building and grounds. His selection and authorization for payroll shall follow the proper channels including the approval of the bishop and the proper paper work through the trustee board and the finance office.

As the Chief Operations Officer, C. O. O., he is the contact person for the leasing of Jurisdictional headquarters for special events. Contracts for work for the jurisdictional headquarters or other properties shall be channelled through his office. Before entering in contractual obligations, he will follow the proper procedure according to the bylaws of the jurisdiction. Simply stated, he must submit the contract to the bishop and the trustee board. It is then submitted to the commissioner of finance for payment.

THIRD ADMINISTRATIVE ASSISTANT

QUALIFICATIONS

The third administrative assistant must have the ability to delegate authority and respond to superiors. He must also be a pastor or superintendent with at least ten years of experience. In addition, he must be a creative and visionary thinker. He should be a resourceful leader with the ability to speak and write well. Like the others, he should have successful administrative experience and or formal training in business or church administration. This shall include but not be limited to college level courses in administration, certificates from administration seminars, or secular job experience in administration.

Finally, he must have a sound history of support to the jurisdiction. In other words, he must be consistent in Jurisdictional and national reports as well as a tither to the jurisdiction.

DUTIES

The third administrative assistant shall support the Bishop by providing leadership in the development of jurisdictional meetings, conventions, convocations, retreats, etc. Formally, he is the chair of the jurisdictional program committee. This committee is appointed by him and must be approved by the bishop. He is also to submit all plans for programs to the bishop for approval prior to implementation.

This assistant is to organize and coordinate the arrangements for guests of the jurisdiction, including speakers for conventions. He is to work within the budget, and the parameters of the provisions of the trustee board and commissioner of finance. . In other words, he is not to promise or arrange for gratuities beyond the resources of the jurisdiction. No arrangements are to be made by him without the prior approval of the bishop.

Finally, the third administrative assistant is to develop and plan for jurisdictional training retreats in concert with the chairman of Christian Education. He is to provide leadership in the scheduling of all jurisdictional meetings including AIM.

RECOMMENDATIONS AND GUIDELINES

1. Numerical designation does not suggest that a given assistant is next in the line of ascension to the office of Jurisdictional Bishop.

2. All assistants serve on the executive board of the jurisdiction, and are considered a key component of the administration.

3. These assistants rank higher than any other jurisdictional officer including superintendents and department heads. In this regard, they are afforded the courtesy and respect of their office.

4. Administrative assistants shall be made privy to decisions of the Bishop prior to disclosure to others. Therefore, they have the responsibility to keep such information confidential until given permission to release the same.

These administrative assistants must have a servant's heart and a willing spirit. They are to work for the good of the jurisdiction in general, and the Bishop in particular.

THE JURISDICITONAL EXECUTIVE BOARD

The Jurisdictional executive board shall henceforth be comprised of the Jurisdictional Administrative Assistants and the Jurisdictional Bishop as the President.

There shall be a person designated to personally manage vendor stands allowed during events at the Jurisdictional Headquarters. The Jurisdictional Prelate and report to the Commissioner of Finance or the Jurisdictional Bishop as directed shall appoint him.

General Duties:
1. Supervise the vendors during Jurisdictional meetings and or any event held at the Jurisdictional Headquarters.

2. Collect fees and report the same to the office of Commissioner of Finance.

4. Keep records of all transactions.

5. Report the need for repairs or maintenance to the Commissioner of Facilities

THE COUNCIL OF SUPERINTENDENTS

The council of superintendents consists of all of the appointed superintendents of districts within the jurisdiction. The chairman of the Superintendents' Council shall provide leadership on behalf of the Jurisdictional Bishop.

General Duties:

1. Identify issues related to all District Superintendents.

2. Organize the council and identify its agenda.

3. Provide leadership among the superintendents in resolving problems of Superintendents.

4. Provide leadership in training new superintendents.

5. He shall be an experienced pastor.

Specific Responsibilities:

1. Conduct workshops and seminars for the training of Superintendents.

2. Identify resources (persons, materials, literature, etc.) for training.

3. Oversee the visitation of Superintendents travel over their districts and report any problems or concerns to the Jurisdictional Bishop.

4. Provide leadership in scheduling and coordinating meetings of districts for the year.

5. Oversee the success of the Superintendents in collecting Jurisdictional and national reports.

6. Lead the Superintendents in including the District Missionaries in the discharge of duties as identified in the Women's Department Handbook.

7. Support the Bishop's program and communicate the program to the Superintendents' Council.

DISTRICT SUPERINTENDENTS

There shall be superintendents to assist the Bishop with the churches in his jurisdiction. Therefore, the District Superintendent is appointed by the jurisdictional Bishop to supervise or give direction to the pastors of local churches under his assignment. Persons in this position serve at the pleasure of the Jurisdictional Bishop.

General Duties:

1   Be available for assistance to pastors in the district.

2   Provide leadership to pastors in the support of the vision and directive of the jurisdiction through the prelate

Specific Duties:

1. Travel through the district in order to oversee the spiritual and temporal affairs of the churches.

2. Provide leadership to all evangelists and local pastors of the district in the

absence and with the directive of the Bishop.

3. Inform the pastors and churches of the district of their duties to the local church, district and national work.

4. Provide counsel with the pastors of the district regarding their pastoral responsibilities when needed.

5. Preside over the annual District Meeting and encourage the members of the district meeting to support their local churches with their faithful attendance and finance and maintain a working and effective fellowship among its pastors.

6. Assist the Bishop in collecting the finances for district, jurisdictional and national work as directed by the Bishop.

7. Provide leadership in mediating disputes involving the pastor and members upon the request of the pastor. If arbitration is needed, the Superintendent shall then commission

an investigating committee to hear the dispute or grievance.

8. The District Superintendent shall be one of the members of this committee unless there is a conflict of interest. The findings shall be reported to the office of the Bishop in writing for disposition.

9. Take charge of a local church within the district at the discretion of the Jurisdictional Bishop, if the pastor dies, resigns, becomes incapacitated, or is removed, until another pastor can be appointed by the Bishop.

10. Where Jurisdictional or national monies have been used to build or buy a church, the District Superintendent shall see that all charters, deeds and other conveyances or church property to his district conform to the discipline and laws of the church, county Jurisdictional or country within which such property is situated.

11. Promote all the interest of the church within his district with the district with the cooperation of the pastors.

CHAIRMAN OF THE PASTORS' AND ELDERS' COUNCIL

The Elders' Council shall consist of all ordained elders who are in good standing with their local churches. The primary function of this organization is that of an appellate body. Therefore, it shall consider matters that are referred to it according to the guidelines of the national church.

General Duties:

1. Identify issues related to pastors and elders.

2. Chair the Elder's Council.

3. Organize the council, identify its agenda, and communicate the same to the members prior to the meeting.

4. Provide leadership among the pastors in resolving problems or concern to them.

5. Certify or have the parliamentarian certify the house for a predetermined quorum prior to each meeting.

6. He shall be an ordained elder.

Specific Responsibilities:

1. Be an ordained Elder in the Church of God in Christ (not a superintendent).

2. Place on the agenda matters that are referred to the Elder's Council by the Jurisdictional Assembly, the Bishop, or other Department Heads for deciding the policies and procedures for conducting Jurisdictional business.

3. Submit a report of its decisions to the appropriate bodies.

4. Chair the trial and/or hearing of cases referred to the Elders' Council under the Constitution of the Church of God in Christ.

5. Allow but monitor the presence of non-ordained ministers attending the Council meetings and make certain that they do not participate in decision-making activities such as debate or voting.

THE BOARD OF TRUSTEES

The Trustee Board is involved in the ministry of the management of jurisdictional properties and operations. They are to hold in "trust" legal documents of property and other business and assist the administration in budget development and the monitoring of financial matters of the organization. The Trustee board shall consist of a Chairman, Vice-Chairman, Secretary, Assistant Secretary, and the Finance Committee.

The Jurisdictional Assembly shall elect the Board of Trustees from its membership. It shall consist of not less than seven (7) and not more than fifteen (15) members and shall hold office for a period of four (4) years or until their successors are elected and qualified.

General Duties:

1. Manage the general financial affairs of the Jurisdiction.

2. Monitor and follow the adopted policies and procedures for fiscal management.

3. Holds in trust all deeds and legal documents of the Jurisdiction.

4. Assist the Bishop and/or the Commissioner of Finance in budget development.

5. Monitor and implement the budget approved by the Jurisdictional Assembly.

6. The chairman shall be an ordained elder or if female, she shall be duly licensed.

Specific Responsibilities:

1. Hold in trust for the use and benefit of the Jurisdiction all deeds to Jurisdictional properties and unused church properties and other such property (ies) as shall be acquired.

2. Hold in trust for the use and benefit of the Jurisdiction any assets which shall become property of the Jurisdiction either by gift, deed, or otherwise, with or without legal designation.

3. Receive from the Bishop or the Commissioner of Finance the parameters for the budget and suggested funds required.

4. Resubmit the above with recommendations as to the resources available to implement.

5. Work with the department heads to determine their contributions to the general Jurisdictional budget.

6. Work in cooperation with the Finance Committee to collect and deposit revenue, and maintain a copy of the budgets of the departments.

7. Receive and approve, if appropriate, the budgets of the departments and auxiliaries of the Jurisdiction including the Department of Women.

8. Upon approval of the Bishop, order and report the results of an annual audit of the finances of the jurisdiction via certified accountants

9. Annually assess all properties of the jurisdiction and make recommendations to the administration.

10. Determine ways and means to supplement budget needs.

11. Participate in and complete a designated seminar or course in finance management.

12. Meet on the third week of each month to carry out the above duties.

FINANCE COMMITTEE:

This group shall serve as the primary banking committee for the Jurisdiction. They shall be appointed to serve by the Jurisdictional Bishop from the recommendations of the Commissioner of Finance. The Financial Secretary from the Commissioner of Finance office shall serve as the secretary of this committee. Their primary duties consist of collecting offerings and depositing the same. They shall also maintain records of revenues received from all sources.

General Duties:

1. Oversee the monthly budget and pay expenses of the Jurisdiction according to the guidelines of policies and procedures for fiscal responsibility.

2. Do not pay any expenses other than those designated without prior approval of the Bishop. Collect offerings in Jurisdictional meetings.

3. Depositing and keeping files and records of the same.

4. Write checks for the disbursement of funds as designated by the Trustee Board.

5. Keep accurate records of other Jurisdictional revenue deposited through the Commissioner of Finance's office.

6. The chairman shall be an ordained elder or if female, duly licensed.

OFFICERS OF THE FINANCE COMMITTEE

In addition to the Commissioner o Finance, there shall be a Financial Secretary and a Jurisdictional Treasurer. Their duties are described as follows:

FINANCIAL SECRETARY

The Secretary of Finance shall maintain records of all financial reports, funds received and disbursed. He or She shall perform such other duties as may be assigned by the Commissioner of Finance or the Jurisdictional Bishop.

The Secretary of Finance shall also be authorized to establish a clerical staff to aid and assist in the discharge of duties with the approval of the Jurisdictional Bishop.

TREASURER

The Jurisdictional Treasurer shall receive all monies and securities of the Jurisdiction and shall make an accounting of all transactions to the Commissioner of Finance. In addition to being appointed by the Jurisdictional Bishop, he shall have the privilege of appointing other persons to assist in the discharge of his duties with the approval of the Bishop.

FINANCIAL POLICIES AND PROCEDURES

According to the job description of the Trustee Board, they are involved in the ministry of the management and distribution of Jurisdictional funds. The specifics of the terms management and distribution are not clearly delineated. Although pages 14 and 15 of the official guidelines^ explain the specific duties, the exact role of the Commissioner of Finance^ is not specified. The Commissioner's role is one of advice and supervision as it relates to the Trustee Board. However, it seems necessary to further clarify the specifics of such interaction to avoid confusion and miscommunication. Therefore, the following policies and procedures are described below and follows:

PROCEDURE ONE: RECEIVING AND DEPOSITING FUNDS

1. All monies are deposited and transactions conducted through one checking account.

2. Monies received through offerings and / or collected during Jurisdictional events are counted by a committed of no less than three (3) and recounted and verified with signatures of no less than two (2) members of the Financial Committee.

3. These funds are recorded on envelopes labeled

according to the group turning them in i.e. Name of District or Name of Jurisdictional Department.

4. The envelope includes a record of the date of the turn in and the signature of the person making the deposit.

5. Items received through the mail are recorded in similar fashion with the name of the person sending it in with the initial of the person recording the information.

6. The second committee will then make a deposit slip for the bank

7. This deposit slip is received and verified by the Jurisdictional Treasurer who in turn makes the actual deposit in the bank.

8. A composite data sheet is prepared by the Jurisdictional Treasurer, which includes all the names of persons and departments and or districts included in the deposit.

9. This composite sheet is given to the Trustee Board and the Commissioner of Finance as verification of funds deposited and available according to banking policy.

10. This data is placed in the computer

PROCEDURE TWO: DISTRIBUTION OF FUNDS

1. The Trustee Board shall meet at least monthly or more often if necessary for the payment of Jurisdictional debts and obligations.

2. The Commissioner of Finance shall receive and submit to the Trustee Board all indebtedness mailed or submitted to the jurisdiction.

3. Budgeted items shall be paid upon approval of the Trustee Board as specified.

4. Non-budgeted items shall be paid according to the guidelines.

5. Other requests for funds shall be submitted to the Commissioner of Finance via voucher.

6. Said voucher shall include the name of the person requesting payment, department or budget category of the request (i.e. maintenance), and receipt (if for reimbursement) or work order for services rendered.

7. The Commissioner of Finance will submit this to the Chairman of the Trustee Board for

8. Payment at the next Board meeting

9. If the payment submitted requires immediate payment, the Commissioner of Finance, the Chairman of the Board of Trustees and the Bishop shall approve the voucher for immediate payment if funds are available.

10. Such transactions shall be brought to the next Trustee Board meeting for retroactive approval.

11. No reimbursement shall be made without prior approval of the Trustee Board for purchase.

PROCEDURES

BUDGETED EXPENDITURES OF $1 TO $399

The procedures of implementing this policy shall be as follows:

1. The organization, auxiliary, committee, authorized individual wishing to make an expenditure shall submit the request to the Commissioner of Finance who, upon verifying the availability of funds, shall approve the request.

2. The Finance Secretary will issue a purchase order (for material goods) or check request (for earmarked funds of an auxiliary) to the Secretary of Finance indicating the expense has been authorized.

3. A check will be issued and the receipt of purchase shall be returned to the Finance Committee to be matched with the purchase order.

BUDGETED EXPENDITURES OF $400 OR MORE

1. The organization, committee, or individual wishing to make an expenditure shall submit the request to the Commissioner of Finance to verify availability of funds.

2. The Commissioner of Finance will approve the request before submitting a purchase order to the Secretary of Finance.

3. The Commissioner of Finance will present the request to the Trustee Board for approval.

4. After approval by the Trustee Board and Bishop, a purchase order will be issued and the expenditure made.

NONBUDGETED EXPENDITURES
(Emergency and Discretionary Expenses)

1. The organization, committee, or individual wishing to make an expenditure shall submit a request along with a written proposal to justify the expenditure to the Finance Committee.

2. The Finance Committee, upon verifying availability of funds, shall approve the request and submit it along with the written proposal to the Trustee Board.

3. The Trustee Board will make a decision as to the appropriateness of the request, and if approved, submit the request to the Bishop.

4. After approval by the Bishop, purchase order will be issued and the expenditure made.

Please understand that these Policies and Procedures shall be reviewed annually for their applicability to the needs of the Jurisdiction and modified accordingly.

SUMMARY OF FINANCIAL POLICIES OF THE JURISDICTION

1.   All Jurisdictional monies will be deposited in the same banking account.

2.   The exception to the above will be the Bishop's Discretionary Fund.

3.   However, monies for the Discretionary Fund shall be received in the main checking account.

4.   A check will be written to the Bishop's Fund as determined by the   Jurisdictional budget.

5.   All expenses allocated to the Jurisdictional Bishop such as travel expenses shall come through the Jurisdictional general account for accounting purposes.

6.   No checks will be written without two signatures.

7.   No blank checks will be issued without prior written approval, via voucher, of the Trustee Board and the Bishop.

8.   Auxiliaries and Departments may maintain their individual checking accounts.

9.   However, a financial statement of the activities of the individual accounts shall be submitted to the Trustee Board on a quarterly basis (A copy of bank statements will suffice).

10.   The Trustee Board, Commissioner of Finance, The Jurisdictional Bishop and Administrative Assistants shall meet quarterly for a review of financial activities. The Chairman of the Trustee Board shall chair this meeting.

ORDINATION BOARD

General Duties:

1. Receive applications for ordination and certify their completeness including verification of coursework from the C.H. Mason Bible College and a letter of recommendation from the pastor of the candidate.
2. Examine all prerequisite qualifications of the candidate.
3. Publicize the requirements of the board to the pastors in the Jurisdiction.
4. Develop procedures for the official examination as well as the general areas of its content and report the same to the candidates.
5. Develop written and oral procedures for a pre-examination of candidates.
6. Develop continuity from the bible college coursework and actual ordination assuring that the

content of the examination reflects both the constitution and doctrine of the Church of God in Christ as outlined in the official manual.

7. All recommendations of the Ordination Board must be approved by the Bishop of the Jurisdiction prior to notifying the candidates of the same.

8. Develop the format and program for the ordination service.

9. Serve a term of office concurrent with that of the administration.

10. The Chairman is to be appointed by the Bishop and members are to be selected from ordained Elders and/or Superintendents.

---

[1] Perry, Bishop Enoch, *Church of God in Christ Sexual Misconduct Policy,* Church of God in Christ Publishing House, 2007.

ADMINISTRATIVE POLICIES

AND PROCEDURES FOR THE

ECCLESIASTICAL JURISDICTION

SEXUAL MISCONDUCT POLICIES[1]

The Ecclesiastical Jurisdiction expects proper Biblically based sexual conduct and behavior of all its members and leaders. However, The Ecclesiastical Jurisdiction expects and requires of its leaders (compensated and volunteer) the highest Biblically based and prescribed standards in sexual behavior. Sexual harassment and/or sexual misconduct by any of the leaders of Ecclesiastical Jurisdiction will result in dismissal, dis-fellowship, and/or referral to appropriate civil authorities as determined by the Ecclesiastical Jurisdiction leaders and members and, if necessary, as determined by the Church of God in Christ, Inc., denomination, and according to the laws of the Jurisdictional of Oklahoma.

I. **Statement of Purpose:**

To outline policy and procedures on Sexual Harassment, Sexual Misconduct, Defamation and Inappropriate Association by employees (compensated or volunteer) and members of Ecclesiastical Jurisdiction expects all its leaders and members alike to refrain from engaging in any conduct that would be viewed or determined to be sexual harassment, sexual misconduct, defamation or inappropriate association. When supportable allegations of sexual harassment, sexual misconduct or defamation arise, (after investigative inquiry by jurisdictional leadership, and if necessary by the Church of God in Christ, Inc.) that allegation will be referred to the appropriate civil authorities for prosecution if deemed appropriate. Any employee (compensated or volunteer) determined to be responsible for sexually harassing behavior, sexual misconduct, action which proves to be grievously defaming or an inappropriate association will be dismissed of all jurisdictional responsibilities and may be legally liable for such offenses. Any member of the jurisdiction responsible for sexually harassing behavior, sexual misconduct, action which proves to be grievously defaming or an inappropriate association may, as determined by Jurisdiction leadership and members, be disfellowshipped from this jurisdiction. All areas of interest where employment, service or activities are provided, the jurisdiction is deemed covered by this policy.

II.   Concepts and Terms:
A. Sexual Harassment.

When unwelcome sexual advances, requests for sexual favors, and other verbal or physical conduct of a sexual nature constitute sexual harassment as defined by Title VII of the Civil Rights Act of 1964.

1.   Quid Pro Quo - When the opportunities of employment, freedoms and service of or in the jurisdiction are conditioned upon submission to sexual demands. Employees shall not engage in any activity that appears to exchange, barter, trade, sell or require maintenance of any employment, service, or activity provided for by the jurisdiction or through one of its contractual agents. Employees or recipients of services shall not be made to believe, feel, or experience the loss of employment or services due to their unwillingness to reciprocate in kind.

2. Hostile (Working) Environment - When the purpose or effect of an individual's conduct creates an environment, which unreasonably interferes with another's work performance or ability to enjoy the freedoms and services of or in the jurisdiction. The employees of the jurisdiction shall not engage in nor allow to be established a work or service providing an environment that does not foster the values of Christian service.

3. Gender Based Discrimination - When the opportunities of employment, freedoms and service of or in the jurisdiction are inappropriately determined or allocated inconsistent with COGIC, Inc., policy as a result of gender, such an action or activity will be considered discriminatory. The employees of The jurisdiction and its members at large, consistent with COGIC, Inc., policy shall not engage in any conduct that would restrict the access of opportunities, freedoms and services from other members and nonmembers because of their gender. All members shall enjoy all the provisions, privileges, and properties that the resources of the jurisdiction provide without regard for their gender. The term gender alone as used in this policy is not intended to include sexual preference. Some sexual preferences are inconsistent with Biblically ordained sexual behavior and as such are spiritually opposed.

4. Sexually Explicit Conduct - Any language (explicit or implied), behavior, gesture, or material(s) possessed by an employee, in the presence of another (especially a teenager or child) that is sexually oriented or conveys an idea sexual in nature will not be condoned. This also includes adult-to-adult romantic or intimate communication in the near presence of a teenager or child without regard for his/her attentiveness.

5. Inappropriate Association - Any behavior, conduct or non-Christian relationship (that which is not indicative of service or fellowship) of an adult with a young adult, teenager or child, or of a non-adult and a child whether mutually agreeable or unsolicited is unacceptable and deemed inappropriate. No minor or person of diminished mental reasoning or ability regardless of his/her legal age or maturity shall be considered able to give his/her consent as pertaining to such association. In the furtherance of this policy issue all employees and members will insure that no adult is alone with any minor (excluding immediate family members) anywhere on or in jurisdiction property or at sponsored activities. No teenager is to be alone with any child (excluding immediate family members) twelve years old or younger anywhere on or in jurisdiction property or at sponsored activities. Occasionally a young adult or teen is charged with the care of children (not yet toilet-trained) who require periodic changing. Such changing should take place in the presence of another teen or adult. Young Christians may mistake genuine Christian interest or appreciation for romantic or intimate affection. Therefore, employees (compensated or volunteer) whose duties require interaction with young Christians must take great care in safeguarding their emerging sensibilities by avoiding any suggestive language, conduct, or physical expressions which may cause a mistaken reaction or belief in the young Christian.

B. Sexual Misconduct. Definition: Conduct that would be reasonably considered sexually inappropriate, unacceptable, or offensive by the overwhelming majority of Christians, moral people or the society at large.

1. Consensual - Existing (on-going) relationships or those entered into by mutual consent without formalization (marriage) are expressly forbidden between employees of this organization and other members, nonmembers, agents, representatives, unemancipated young adults or other minors. No minor child or person of diminished mental reasoning or ability regardless of his/her legal age or maturity shall be considered able to give his/her consent to disregard this policy.

2. Exposure - The deliberate revealing of the genitals or any other part of the sexual anatomy for the purpose of exploitation, gratification, or intimidation is condemned as unacceptable behavior. Employees should take great care in entering and exiting rest facilities, making adjustment to apparel, or relieving discomfort due to restrictive clothing. Those persons charged with the care of children not yet toilet trained, which requires periodic changing, should do so in approved areas only.

3. Sexual Assault - The aggravated removal of another's clothing as to expose either his/her undergarments or nakedness in the commission or attempted commission of a sexual act (e.g., rape) will be reported to legal authorities for investigation and prosecution. Persons engaged in assisting the less able, whether they are young or infirm, should not provide any assistance unless the individual is clearly unable to remove his/her outer garments (coats, jackets, or sweaters) for himself/herself. When such assistance is necessary, it should be undertaken with such care as not to imply any inappropriate behavior.

4. Sexual Battery - The unlawful and unwanted touching, fondling, deliberate offensive contact of a sexual nature, implied or gestured, and or groping (aggravated looking in a lewd manner) of a person's sexual anatomy is illegal and will not be tolerated. Under this policy minors cannot consent and all behavior with any minor or unemancipated young adult is unlawful and unwanted.

5. Defamation: To do damage or harm, verbally or in writing, to the character or reputation of an individual with or without knowledge or intent.

6. Slander - When an employee (compensated or volunteer) communicates to others verbally information of a sexual or non-sexual nature that proves to be false and that communication causes injury (emotional, physical or financial) to that person or his/her reputation. The jurisdiction acknowledges that all employees shall hold all such information regardless of its merit in the strictest confidence. The trust endeared to the jurisdiction and its representatives by confession, counseling, written conveyance, or casual conversation should never be repeated unless permission of the member or parties has been given. Persons who conduct conversations that border on (but are not legally) slander will be counseled, warned (as an attempt to correct), or terminated from either employment or appointment after repeated violation. The sanctity of privileged communication does not extend to third parties. If the representative believes that a third party, such as a parent, has a vested interest in the information received during confession, counseling, written conveyance, or casual conversation, that representative should counsel that individual to inform his/her or seek the guidance of jurisdiction officials.

6.   Libel - When an employee (compensated or volunteer) communicates to others verbally or in writing false information of a sexual or non-sexual nature intended to give an unfavorable impression of another person, and that communication causes injury (emotional, physical or financial) to that person or his/her reputation. The jurisdiction requires all written communication (hand or electronic) done on its behalf to be approved before release (in publication, mailings, personal exchange, or electronic transmission). Employees should not keep, dictate, and record any information that by accidental release would be viewed as demeaning. Employees will not draw, depict in likeness, effigy or caricature any person in any way that could reasonably be considered unfavorable.

III.   Organization:

A. Ecclesiastical Jurisdiction, Inc. The incorporated organization recognized as Oklahoma Southeast Jurisdiction COGIC, or herein called the jurisdiction, is comprised of its ministries, auxiliaries, fellowships, groups, missions, or sponsored activities under the direction of its constituted or representative agents carrying out its spiritual mandates or legal responsibilities.

B. Affected Persons.

1.   Compensated Employee - Those persons who receive wages (hourly) or salary (annual or percentage rate) on a regularly recurring basis. This excludes those persons who may receive honoraria or repayment for expenditures made on behalf of the jurisdiction.

2. Appointed Non-Compensated Ministerial Staff/Credential Holders appointed to supervisory positions of leadership in the jurisdiction - These persons receive no compensation for work or in kind labor compensation, although they may receive per diem for jurisdiction related business to cover the cost of the activity. These supervisory leaders may also receive honoraria related to special singular events. Persons in this category are appointed, non-compensated employees or agents.

3. Appointed Non-Compensated Non-Ministerial and Volunteer - A non-credentialed member appointed to a supervisory position or appointed to provide a service to the general membership of the jurisdiction. These persons normally do not receive per diem or honoraria, but may be reimbursed for expenses made on behalf of the jurisdiction by their activity. Persons in this category are appointed non-compensated employees or agents.

4. **Contractual Agent and Contractual Service Providers** - A contractual agent is one with whom the jurisdiction has a continuous contractual relationship whereby the agent represents the jurisdiction to the public. While in the fulfillment of this contract the agent will abide by this policy. The agent remains unencumbered other than in a moral sense when not in direct representation. A contractual Service Provider is one who provides a one-time point of service until the conclusion of a term. While such a provider is rendering services to or on behalf of Oklahoma Southeast Jurisdiction COGIC, the service contractor will be made aware of this policy and contractually be required to comply with its tenets during the terms of the service provision. However, any moral indifference to this policy may be reason to terminate the contractual relationship.

5. Community Service Workers - Persons who are allowed to perform Court- directed community service work. They provide non-compensated labor to the jurisdiction and, therefore, to the community by performing general service to the jurisdiction. Although these individuals are under the direct control of an on site supervisor, their work on jurisdiction property subjects them to this policy. The representative of the jurisdiction is responsible for informing these workers and enforcing the policy.

IV. **Appointment Process:** Due to the seriousness of Sexual Harassment/Sexual Misconduct, it is necessary to follow certain procedures in appointing non-compensated personnel. The Investigation Committee will be responsible for leveling and weighing any findings. The following points of interest may or may not be part of the formal employment process for compensated employees, as determined by the Investigation Committee.

1. **Criminal Background Checks**. Inquiry to local law enforcement.

2. **References.** Send a prospective employee reference form to current or previous employers

3. **Drug Testing.** Employees, compensated or appointed, undergo urine or blood test.

4. **DMV Check.** Check of Jurisdictional Motor Vehicle License.

5. **Psychological Screening.** Bishop, Trustees, Department Chairmen, or sensitive administrative positions

6. **Financial Statement.** Simple assets and liabilities statement to assess possible conflicts of interest, unusually high level of indebtedness, or other financial practices that may be incompatible with the considered appointment.

7. **Other information** that the Investigation Committee may find necessary to support candidate's appointment.

Note: It is the intention of the jurisdiction to govern the general membership of the jurisdiction by spiritual precepts and the norms of acceptable Christian behavior. However, any violation of this policy by any member will be reported to the proper authorities for investigation or legal action.

V. PROCEDURES FOR REPORTING SUSPECTED ABUSE OR NEGLECT OF A CHILD OR SPECIAL ADULT

If you have a reason to suspect a staff member, employee/volunteer, or Jurisdiction member has abused or neglected a child in any way; Oklahoma law mandates that you make a report. Any person who suspects or observes any incident of physical, mental or sexual abuse or neglect of a child must immediately take the following steps:

1) If necessary, protect the child.

2) Immediately make a report to:

   a. Locally: The Pastor, Assistant Pastor, Administrative Assistant, Chairman of Investigation Committee, Church Mother or the Pastor's Wife
   b. Jurisdiction: The Jurisdictional Bishop, Administrative Assistant, District

Superintendent, Jurisdictional Secretary, Supervisor of Women or District Missionary

c. Governmental Jurisdictional Department of Protective and Regulatory Services Children's Protective Services (CPS) (if the alleged or suspected abuse involves a person responsible for the care, custody, or welfare of the child), Statewide 24 Hour Hotline (1-800-522-3511).

d. Law Enforcement
Police - 911
Sheriff- 911

e. Attorney for the Jurisdiction

3) Within 24 hours of a report of suspected abuse or neglect of a child or special adult, the Bishop, Chairman of the Council of Pastors and Elders, Investigation Committee (Bishop, Administrative Assistant or Jurisdictional Secretary at the jurisdictional level) and any other professional that may be recommended by any of these persons shall begin to investigate all allegations of inappropriate conduct or relationships. Inappropriate conduct includes violations of these policies.

4) The employee/volunteer may be monitored or reassigned. In cases involving serious allegations, the services of the employee/volunteer will be suspended pending the outcome of the investigation.

The Jurisdiction requires each staff member, employee/volunteer, and jurisdiction member to comply with this law. Protecting the physical, mental, sexual and spiritual well being of our preschoolers, children, youth and special adults is important to our jurisdiction. In order to ensure the protection of the previous groups, the jurisdiction has adopted the procedures in Section VII below for responding to reported allegations.

VI. PROCEDURES FOR REPORTING SUSPECTED SEXUAL HARASSMENT/SEXUAL MISCONDUCT (ADULT TO ADULT)

If you have a reason to suspect a staff member, employee/volunteer, or jurisdiction member has sexually harassed you or committed sexual misconduct, take the following steps:

1) Immediately make a report to:

   a. The Bishop, Administrative Assistant or Jurisdictional Secretary at the jurisdictional level

   b. Bishop, Chairman of the Council of Pastors and Elders and or Chairman of Investigation Committee

   c. On the local level this would include the Pastor, Administrative Assistants, and Chairman of Deacons

2)   Within 24 hours of a report of suspected sexual harassment/sexual misconduct, the Bishop, Chairman of the Council of Pastors and Elders, Investigation Committee and any other professional that may be recommended by any of these persons shall begin to investigate all allegations of inappropriate conduct or relationships. Inappropriate conduct includes violations of these policies.   The employee/volunteer may be monitored or reassigned.   In cases involving serious allegations, the services of the employee/volunteer will be suspended pending the outcome of the investigation.

The Jurisdiction requires each staff member, employee/volunteer, and jurisdiction member to comply with this law. Protecting the physical, mental, sexual and spiritual well being of our staff, volunteers and members is important to our jurisdiction.   In order to ensure the protection of the previous groups, the Jurisdiction has adopted the procedures in Section VII below for responding to reported allegations.

RESPONSE TO SEXUAL HARASSMENT OR SEXUAL MISCONDUCT ALLEGATIONS

A.   RESPONSE PROCEDURES

In case of an actual sexual harassment/sexual misconduct allegation involving jurisdiction staff, employees/volunteers, or members, the following guidelines will be observed:

1. The director of that particular ministry must be notified. All efforts at handling the incident must be documented.

2. The director of that particular ministry must report the incident to the Bishop, the Chairman of the Deacons, and the Chairman of the Investigation Committee.

3. The Bishop, Chairman of the Council of Pastors and Elders and Chairman of the Investigation Committee shall coordinate to insure immediate notification of the parents of the alleged victim(s).

4. The staff shall communicate and work with the alleged victim and his or her parents/guardians.

5. The Bishop, Chairman of the Council of Pastors and Elders, and Chairman of the Investigation Committee shall coordinate to insure that a report of the incident is made immediately to the church insurance company and an Attorney for the Jurisdiction.

6. The accused should not be confronted until the safety of the alleged victim is secured and only upon advisement by an Attorney for the Jurisdiction.

7. After consultation with the Attorney for the Jurisdiction, the Bishop, Chairman of the Council of Pastors and Elders, and Chairman of the Investigation Committee may make a prepared statement to the press and to the congregation.

B. RESPONSE TO THE ALLEGED VICTIM

1. The care and safety of the alleged victim is the first priority.

2. All allegations will be taken seriously.

3. Emotional and spiritual support should be given to the alleged victim.

4. The alleged victim and the alleged victim's family shall be given appropriate resources.

C.   RESPONSE TO THE ALLEGED PERPETRATOR

1. Treat the accused with dignity and respect.

2. He/she will be relieved of his/her duties until the investigation is finished.

3. All information will be held in confidence and disclosed only to those with a need to know.

4. The alleged perpetrator and the alleged perpetrator's family shall be given appropriate resources.

D.   INVESTIGATION

1. The Jurisdictional bishop shall appoint a committee selected from the Jurisdictional Council of Pastors and Elders. The Investigation Committee will conduct a thorough investigation of the situation involving any employee/volunteer (except for the Bishop), with the counsel of designated Attorney for the Jurisdiction. The Bishop, Chairman of the Council of Pastors and Elders, and any other professionals that may be recommended by any of the previous persons, will be involved.

2. The findings and recommendations of the Investigation Committee will be presented to the Bishop for final action.

3. In the case of the Bishop, the Investigation Committee will conduct the investigation, with the counsel of a designated Attorney for the Jurisdiction. The Investigation Committee will present the findings to the Deacons who will make the final decisions.

SEXUAL HARASSMENT/MISCONDUCT POLICY AGREEMENT

I hereby affirm that I have read and understand the Ecclesiastical Jurisdiction Sexual Harassment/ Sexual Misconduct Policy. I agree to adhere to the policies and procedures outlined therein while involved in any capacity for Ecclesiastical Jurisdiction.

NAME (PRINT)

_____

Signature:_____

Date:_____

Response to Sexual Harassment And Sexual Misconduct Allegations

Response Procedures:

In case of an actual sexual harassment / sexual misconduct allegation involving jurisdiction staff, employees/volunteers, or members, the following guidelines will be observed:

1. The director of that particular ministry must be notified. All efforts at handling the incident must be documented.

2. The director of that particular ministry must report the incident to the Bishop, the Chairman of the Deacons, and the Chairman of the Investigation Committee.

3. The Bishop, Chairman of the Council of Pastors and Elders and Chairman of the Investigation Committee shall coordinate to insure immediate notification of the parents of the alleged victim(s).

4. The staff shall communicate and work with the alleged victim and his or her parents/guardians.

5. The Bishop, Chairman of the Council of Pastors and Elders, and Chairman of the Investigation Committee shall coordinate to insure that a report of the incident is made immediately to the church insurance company and an Attorney for the Jurisdiction.

6. The accused should not be confronted until the safety of the alleged victim is secured and only upon advisement by an Attorney for the Jurisdiction.

7. After consultation with the Attorney for the Jurisdiction, the Bishop, Chairman of the Council of Pastors and Elders, and Chairman of the Investigation Committee may make a prepared statement to the press and to the congregation.

Response to the Alleged Victim:

1. The care and safety of the alleged victim is the first priority.

2. All allegations will be taken seriously.

3. Emotional and spiritual support should be given to the alleged victim.

4. The alleged victim and the alleged victim's family shall be given appropriate resources.

Response to Alleged Perpetrator:

1. Treat the accused with dignity and respect.

2. He/she will be relieved of his/her duties until the investigation is finished.

3. All information will be held in confidence and disclosed only to those with a need to know.

4. The alleged perpetrator and the alleged perpetrator's family shall be given appropriate resources.

Investigation:

1. The Jurisdictional bishop shall appoint a committee selected from the Jurisdictional Council of Pastors and Elders. The Investigation Committee will conduct a thorough investigation of the situation involving any employee/volunteer (except for the Bishop), with

the counsel of designated Attorney for the Jurisdiction. The Bishop, Chairman of the Council of Pastors and Elders, and any other professionals that may be recommended by any of the previous persons, will be involved.

2. The findings and recommendations of the Investigation Committee will be presented to the Bishop for final action.

3. In the case of the Bishop being the accused, the Investigation Committee will conduct the investigation, with the counsel of a designated Attorney for the Jurisdiction. The Investigation Committee will present the findings to the Executive Board who will forward the findings to the Chairman of the Board of Bishops.

4. The outcome will be determined by the Grievance Committee of the Board of Bishops and referred to the Presiding Bishop and General Board for final action.

Sexual Misconduct Review Board

There shall be a sexual misconduct review board for the Jurisdiction. This board shall be hand selected by the Jurisdictional Bishop, and serve at his discretion or unless there is a conflict of interest in any particular case brought before it. In such cases the member of the board in question shall recluse himself from the case and replaced by an alternate on a temporary basis by the Jurisdictional Bishop or his designee.

The primary purpose of the Sexual Misconduct Review Board is to conduct a comprehensive assessment and review of all information and documentation provided in response to allegations of sexual misconduct against the accused.

In no case will any participant in connection with an investigation before the Sexual Misconduct Review Board disclose any information regarding Review Board discussions, accused/accuser/witness information, testimony, or printed documentation outside of the Review Board's proceedings.

In no case will any participant in any way divulge, copy, release, sell, loan, review, alter or destroy any confidential information in connection with an investigation before the Sexual Misconduct Review Board.

In no case will any participant misuse confidential information obtained in connection with a matter being investigated before the Sexual Misconduct Review Board.

It is understood that a participant has no right or ownership interest in any confidential information referred to in this Agreement.

Convicted Ex-Sex Offender in Church

The following steps shall be taken when a convicted sex offender wants to attend church or becomes a member of the church:

1. Obtain a record of the offender's prior criminal convictions.

2. Obtain the conditions of the sex offender's parole requirements in writing.
   a. Obtain more specific conditions from the parole officer for the offender.
   b. If he or she is free to attend church, what are the stipulations?

3. Condition the sex offender's right to attend church services and activities on his or her signing a conditional attendance agreement as follows:
   a. The offender will not work with minors in any capacity in the church
   b. He or she will not transport minors to or from church or any church activity
   c. The sex offender will not attend any youth or children's functions while on

church property only if in the presence of a chaperone.

d. The sex offender will not visit the toilet facilities without an assigned escort.

e. A single violation of these conditions will result in an immediate termination of the sex offender[s privilege to attend the church.

4. The sex offender will be given and required to sign the church's sexual misconduct and harassment policy.

DEPARTMENT OF WOMEN

JURISDICTIONAL SUPERVISOR OF THE DEPARTMENT OF WOMEN

The Jurisdictional Supervisor of the Department of Women shall preside over the Department of Women of said Jurisdiction. One of the prime objectives of the Jurisdictional Supervisor is to work in harmony and agreement with the Jurisdictional Bishop to the best of her ability and to organize the Department of Women in the Jurisdiction. She shall be responsible for the organization of every auxiliary and unit that has been handed down to her by the General Supervisor of the Department of Women with the approval of the Jurisdictional Bishop

The program of the Jurisdictional Supervisor shall be that as presented to her by the General Supervisor and she is not to inject any personal attitude that would destroy the program that is assigned to her to promote.

General Duties:

1. Organize the work of this department in with the goals and objectives of the Bishop.

2. Supervise the general operation of the department including the development of and implementation of its budget.

3. Promote Jurisdictional and National programs.

4. Make periodic visits to the districts providing encouragement and correction as needed.

5. Oversee the training of all workers for this department.

6. Appoint staff and personnel to assist in carrying out the program of the Jurisdictional and national work.

7. Obtain license from the office of the General Supervisor and issue Certificates of Appointments for women appointees, with the approval of the Jurisdictional Prelate.

8. Issue license in the Jurisdiction to all eligible women for Jurisdictional and district recognition

and as otherwise authorized by the General Supervisor of the Department of Women.

9. Assure the collection and reporting of all reports for Women's Department Auxiliaries, units and for women credential-holders.

10. Supervise and support the work of the District Missionaries.

DISTRICT MISSIONARIES

General Duties:

1. Preside over the district in the interest of affecting a full setup of auxiliaries in each church and interest in women in women's work.

2. Keep well informed in all areas of women's work.

3. Support the programs identified by the Jurisdictional Supervisor of the Department of Women.

4. Work in harmony with and support the work of the District Superintendent of the area in which she is assigned.

5. Work in harmony with the pastors of her district by securing permission for conducting activities with their membership and in their churches.

6. Utilize their influence to encourage women to attend the Jurisdictional and national Women's Conventions.

7. Be an advisor and a friend to the Church Mothers in the district.

8. Provide leadership in encouraging financial support of the Jurisdictional and national among the women in the district.

9. Provide leadership in the collection and reporting of Jurisdictional and national reports of the Women's Department.

AUXILIARIES IN MINISTRY (A.I.M.)

The auxiliaries of the jurisdiction are identified as Auxiliaries in Ministry (A.I.M.). It consists of the five (5) traditional departments of the Church, namely; Sunday School, Youth (Young People's Willing Workers-YPWW), Missions, Evangelism and Music. They exist on the international, jurisdictional, district and local levels of operation. The officers are appointed by the jurisdictional Bishop. All departments of the jurisdiction shall support the financial program of the jurisdiction as well as the international body to which it is associated.

A.I.M. CHAIRPERSON

The Jurisdictional Chair of A.I.M. may or may not have the sole position in many jurisdictions. Some may hold one of the offices of an auxiliary. However, due to the magnitude of responsibility, the international leadership recommends that effective functioning, as chair is when it is their only responsibility.

Jurisdictional A.I.M. Chair Responsibilities[2]:

1. The Chair is directly responsible to the Jurisdictional Bishop for the successful functioning of this area of ministry.
2. Give leadership to fulfilling the vision of the Jurisdictional Bishop.
3. Oversee the effective organization and development of the Departments.
4. Chair the A.I.M. committee for the annual convention or conference.
5. Give leadership to the annual President's Banquet.
6. Meet with the department leaders for monitoring progress and development of this ministry.
7. Give leadership to financial development of the departments.
8. The Chairperson of A.I.M. is the team leader for success, motivation and development of all leaders of this department.
9. The Chair shall give leadership in the training of workers of A.I.M. at the jurisdictional and district levels.
10. Pray for the effectiveness of this ministry.

---

[2] Gilkey, Supt. Mark, et.al. **Jurisdictional Auxiliaries in Ministry Convention Handbook**, 3rd edition, MLG Ministries, Wichita, Kansas, 2013.

SUNDAY SCHOOL DEPARTMENT

The Sunday School Department shall be for the training and enlightening of children and adults in scriptural understanding of the doctrines of the Church of God in Christ. At the Jurisdictional level, it shall be under the direction of the Jurisdictional Sunday School Superintendent who shall be appointed by the Bishop of the Jurisdiction. He / She shall be in good standing morally and financially with the Jurisdiction.

The Jurisdictional Superintendent of the Sunday School shall supervise the work of the Sunday School in the Jurisdiction of his appointment. He shall organize and set up the Sunday School Department at the Jurisdictional level by establishing Sunday School Districts therein, and shall supervise the Sunday School on the Jurisdictional and district levels.

There shall also be a Jurisdictional Sunday School Representative. She shall assist the Sunday School Superintendent in the discharge of his duties. She shall not organize any program without the approval of the Superintendent. All persons in this department are under the immediate supervision of the Jurisdictional Bishop and shall work in cooperation with the activities of the Department of Education. The specific duties of the officers of this department are the same as those found in the national manual for the department.

Other officers of this department shall consist of an Assistant Superintendent, Secretary, Assistant Secretary, Treasurer, Devotional Leader and Sunday School Teachers. It is the duty of the Superintendent to oversee the development of Sunday School Workers in every district of the jurisdiction. More specifically the Jurisdictional Superintendent shall fulfil the following assignments with the approval of the Bishop:

1. Organize and recommend all officers of the department.

2. Oversee the development Sunday School staff in every district with the approval of the district superintendent.

3. Supervise the various programs of the department

4. Supervise and develop the annual budget for this department

5. Be responsible for the financial obligations of the department to the jurisdiction and international department of Sunday School.

6. Participate in the Jurisdictional and International A.I.M Conventions.

7. Provide opportunities to train all Sunday School workers

8. Collaborate with the Department of Education for ongoing educational programs for teachers and workers.

Criteria for Selection of Department Staff:

Jurisdictional Level. All staff serves at the pleasure of the Jurisdictional Bishop. He has the right, at any time, to appoint and/or remove without notice. All staff at this level should also be in good standing in his/her local and district. The request to serve at this level must first be approved by the individual's pastor.

District Level. All staff serves at the pleasure of the District Superintendent, who serves at the pleasure of the Jurisdictional Bishop. He has the right, at any time, to appoint and/or remove without notice. All staff at this level should also be in good standing in his/her local church. If you desire an individual to work at the district level, his/her pastor must first, approve the request.

Local Level. All staff serves at the pleasure of the pastor. The pastor has the right, at any time, to appoint and/or remove without notice. All staff at this level should be in good standing in the church (supporting the pastor and vision of the church with his/her attendance and finances). If you desire an individual to work at the local level, the pastor must first, approve the request.

THE DEPARTMENT OF YOUTH

THE YOUNG PEOPLE'S WILLING WORKERS (Y.P.W.W.)

The Y.P.W.W. Department shall be for the training and enlightening of children and adults in scriptural understanding of the doctrines of the Church of God in Christ. At the Jurisdictional level, it shall be under the direction of the Y.P.W.W. President who shall be appointed by the Bishop of the Jurisdiction. He/She shall be in good standing morally and financially with the Jurisdiction.

The Jurisdictional Y.P.W.W. President shall supervise the work of the Y.P.W.W. in the Jurisdiction of his appointment. Therefore, he shall set up the Willing Worker in said Jurisdiction by organizing the same in the districts of the Jurisdictional.

He shall, also supervise the Y.P.W.W. on the Jurisdictional and district levels. The president shall recommend a female to the Bishop for approval as the Y.P.W.W. Chairlady. The chairlady shall assist the President and shall not develop or organize programs in this department without his approval and the approval of the Jurisdictional Bishop. All persons in this department are under the immediate supervision of the Jurisdictional Bishop and shall work in cooperation with the activities of the Department of Education. The specific duties of the officers of this department are the same as those found in the national manual for the department.

In conjunction with the directives of the International Youth Department, the Department of Youth adheres to the following directives[3]:

A. Mission

The Youth Department will use innovative methods to insure that our youth become valued resources to their families, churches, and communities. We will teach them how to become self-sustaining productive citizens. This department will pursue financial resources that will allow it to cultivate opportunities for the church's young to become economically empowered and producers of jobs in the body of Christ, without compromising Godly principles. The expected out come is producing law-abiding outstanding youth to become agents of change in our church and society.

Visionary Goals

It is the goal of the Youth Department in the Church of God in Christ to enhance the lives of its members, both naturally and spiritually, thereby equipping them to successfully confront their present challenges, and those in the years to come. This goal will be achieved by producing informative and innovative techniques via conventions, youth rallies,

---

[3] http://www.cogic.org/iyd

etc., designed to address the existing issues concerning our youth, and their current circumstances.

The leadership of the Youth Department will actively and aggressively seek talent within the church necessary to bring these goals to fruition maintaining dignity, Christian purpose, and integrity.

Objectives

The Youth Department of the Church of God in Christ will perpetuate an equipping ministry of excellence to prepare our youth for worldwide ministry. Each and every member of our department will function as concerned, skilled, youth leaders to carry out the vision of this department, and enable our youth to live Godly and fulfilling lives.

The Youth Department of the Church of God in Christ is a vibrant training auxiliary that exists to equip our youth with the necessary training to live a prosperous and victorious life in Jesus Christ. This charismatic department will design, develop, and implement programs and ministry opportunities that meet the spiritual needs of the youth of our church. Rallies, workshops, and pertinent seminars will be tools used to effectively teach our youth how to apply the Word of God in their lives.

THE DEPARTMENT OF MISSIONS

There shall be a Department of Missions for the spiritual and doctrinal development of Missions in underdeveloped areas in both local and foreign territories. There shall be a president and an elect lady. The president shall have the primary responsibility for the organization of this department. The elect lady shall work in cooperation with the president. She shall not organize programs within this department without his approval and the approval of the Jurisdictional Bishop. The specific duties of the officers of this department are the same as those found in the national manual for the department[4].

Vision Statement: To reach the lost with the Gospel of Jesus Christ and provide relief for the suffering at home and around the world.

The Mission of the Missions Department:

1. To promote and support the vision of the jurisdiction for domestic and global missions projects.
2. To educate, train, and develop preachers and missionaries in all aspects of missions work
3. To continue the progression of the preaching of the gospel in foreign countries, especially in areas where there are no missionaries and areas where sound doctrine is not being preached

[4] www.cogic.org/missions

4. To assist in the completion of the existing missions projects of the jurisdiction.

5. To provide leadership in addressing disaster relief within the geographical region of the jurisdiction and beyond.

6. To improve the efforts for obtaining better financial support for the foreign works while lessening the struggle. The accomplishment of this specific goal, upon which the other goals are hinged, will be a direct result of a reasonable budget allocated for mission work.

7. To promote home missions by encouraging the local church to do the following:

> a) Engage in activities to build/restore the family unit
>
> b) Engage in missions and development of the community
>
> c) Engage in active street, prison, and nursing home ministries
>
> d) Commit to the financial support of the National Missions Department

Goals

1. To educate, train, and develop preachers and missionaries in all aspects of mission work;

2. To continue the progression of the preaching of the gospel in foreign countries, especially in areas where

there are no missionaries and areas where sound doctrine is not being preached;

3. To engage the youth in the work of missions through Y.O.A.M. (Youth On A Mission).

4. To strengthen jurisdictional and local church growth by assisting districts and churches with missions efforts in concert with the work of outreach and evangelism;

5. To continue conducting periodic visits to the established International Church Sites;

6. To improve the efforts for obtaining better financial support for the foreign works while lessening the struggle.

THE DEPARTMENT OF EVANGELISM

There shall be a Department of Evangelism. This department has the primary responsibility to conduct the evangelical work and program of the Jurisdiction. There shall be a president and an elect lady. The president shall have the primary responsibility for the organization of this department. The elect lady shall work in cooperation with the president. She shall not organize programs within this department without his approval and the approval of the Jurisdictional Bishop. The specific duties of the officers of this department are the same as those found in the national manual for the department.[5]

The following goals are in agreement with the goals of the international Department of Evangelism:

Jurisdictional Level.
1. For every district in the jurisdiction to have a trained, equipped and effective Department of Evangelism.
2. The jurisdictional department shall serve as an immediate resource of training for both the district and for the local church.
3. To recruit, train and lead workers in effective, consistent methods of evangelism.
4. For every jurisdictional worker to be involved and support the jurisdictional A.I.M. functions

District Level.
1. For every district in the jurisdiction to have a trained, equipped and effective Department of Evangelism staff.
2. For the district department to serve as an immediate resource for the local church.
3. To recruit, train and lead workers in effective, consistent methods of evangelism.
4. For every district worker to be involved and support the jurisdictional, regional and international levels of the department.

Local Level.

---

[5] Www.cogic.org/evangelism

1. For each church in the jurisdiction to have a trained, equipped, consistently functioning and effective Department of Evangelism; leading to
   a. The salvation of souls in the church's community and
   b. The growth, in all aspects, of the local church.
2. For every member to support the vision of the pastor by winning souls.
3. For every local worker to be involved and support the district, jurisdictional and International A.I.M.

Additional Goals

1. Carry the saving and healing message of Jesus Christ to every nation and islands of the earth through our evangelists and local churches.

2. For the President to make personal contact with every district president at least once per year.

3. For the Elect Lady to make personal contact with every district elect lady at least once per year.

4. For every district to have a vibrant Department of Evangelism.

5. For all of our churches to have a vibrant Department of Evangelism.

6. For all Ministers, Elders without charge and evangelist missionaries to by virtue of their credentials to be given permission by their pastors to participate with this department.

7. Provide training, information and support through our School of Evangelism for evangelists in the Church Of God In Christ.

THE DEPARTMENT OF MUSIC

There shall be a Department of Music in the Jurisdiction. The Jurisdictional Minister of Music shall head this department. He or she shall be appointed by the Jurisdictional Bishop and shall serve or be replaced at his pleasure. The Minister of Music shall organize choirs and other such musical groups upon the approval of the Bishop. The specific duties of the officers of this department are the same as those found in the national manual for the department.

Vision

1. To centralize the focus of this ministry on Jesus and His kingdom through teaching and mentoring.

2. To equip the constituents of the Jurisdictional Department of Music with tools necessary to minister with excellence and anointing.

Mission

1. To encourage, utilize and bring to the forefront the hidden talents and gifts of those who serve in this department.

2. To support and encourage opportunities which allow each gift to be utilized to its maximum potential.

3. To continually endeavour to make the Jurisdictional Music Department the best it can be in giving glory to the Name of the Lord.

THE JURISDICTIONAL USHER BOARD

There shall be a Jurisdictional Usher Board in the Jurisdiction. A president shall head this department. Other officers may be identified as approved by the Jurisdictional Bishop. He or she shall be appointed by the Jurisdictional Bishop and shall serve or be replaced at his pleasure. This department constitutes the primary ministry of helps in the Jurisdiction. The specific duties of the officers of this department are the same as those found in the national manual for the department.

Our Bible Basis

For a day in thy courts is better than a thousand. I had rather be a doorkeeper in the house of my God, than to dwell in the tents of wickedness. – Psalm 84:10

Our Mission

- Maintain an orderly worship atmosphere in God's house for a positive Christian experience.
- Recruit and train ushers to exhibit excellence at all levels.
- Develop leaders which promote high productivity and professionalism in the Usher ministry.

JURISDICTIONAL ADJUTANCY[6]

CHIEF JURISDICTIONAL ADJUTANT+
The Chief Jurisdictional Adjutant serves at the pleasure of the Bishop. He is responsible for general oversight of all protocol and etiquette within the jurisdiction. He maintains an open line of communication with the Bishop and Administrative staff in an attempt to work and bring harmony to all departments and leaders within the jurisdiction. He selects qualified men and women with the confirmation of the Bishop to serve the adjutancy by regions or districts. Further, he is responsible for all training of the Adjutancy and leadership within the Jurisdiction. He makes certain that all ceremonial and official dress codes are understood and carried out. He also serves as a consultant to pastors and Jurisdictional leaders in areas of protocol, order and programming.

---

[6] Williams, Bishop Matthew, **The National Adjutancy Church of God in Christ, Pocket Guide,** Revised Edition, 2014, Church of God in Christ Publishing House, Memphis, Tennessee, pp.24-26.

General Duties:

1. He is the elder who assists the Jurisdictional Bishop and shall be in service to him.

2. Arrange the general processional in Jurisdictional services and designated ceremonies.

3. Manage the platform.

4. To set up the convention for the service of Holy Communion.

5. Assists the Bishop in administrative details.

Specific Responsibilities:

1. Arrange tables and set them up for communion.

2. Organize the participants for the communion service.

3. Make arrangements for aides to assist in Jurisdictional functions.

4. Assist the Bishop in donning his garments for service.

5. Designate seating arrangements for the platform in Jurisdictional meetings.

6. Organize all Jurisdictional leaders for the processional in Jurisdictional meetings.

7. Assist the Bishop as he directs with his out-of-Jurisdictional guests.

8. Develop and implement the training of Elders for Adjutant service.

Episcopal Adjutant

This is the designated aide to the Jurisdictional Bishop and consults with the Jurisdictional Chief Adjutant to make sure that primary and immediate concerns of the Bishop are met. He must be available to travel with the Bishop, especially within the Jurisdiction. He is also responsible for upkeep and security of the Bishop's vestments.

District / Regional Adjutants

District/Regional Adjutants represent the Jurisdictional Adjutancy whenever the leader's presence is in that particular region or district. They are to make sure that the desires and wishes of the Bishop are adhered to and carried out. This includes: proper transportation, appropriate accommodations and that the required honorarium is provided. They should be knowledgeable of the general duties and wishes of the Jurisdictional Leadership.

DEPARTMENT OF PUBLIC RELATIONS

The Department of Public Relations, (DPR), is a Department attached to the Office of the Jurisdictional Bishop, and functions at his direction. Its mission is to promote the Jurisdictional image, interest and security as identified by the Jurisdictional Bishop, through informing the Jurisdiction, both local and district, and thereby creating a wider understanding of the Jurisdictional Bishop's Vision and policy. The responsibilities can be grouped into three main media areas: broadcasting, print and electronic. The Department of Public (DPR) manages the Jurisdiction's Partnership in the Community, with Volunteer and Businesses.

Jurisdictional Public Relations Officer

The Jurisdictional Public Relations Officer (PRO) serves as the main "voice" of the Jurisdiction only after the approval of the Jurisdictional Bishop. He/she shall, share information with the community about the organization's mission, needs and activities. The PRO works with many audiences, from pastors and congregations to community leaders and the media.

The PRO may be called upon to write newsletters and news releases, handle media outreach, write and lie out brochures and fliers, and issue annual reports. He/She may also prepare scripts for speeches, produce videos, also maintain websites, coordinate special events, manage fundraising, represent the jurisdiction at community gatherings, or respond to public concerns or questions.

General Duties:

1. Oversee the appropriate news releases for the Jurisdiction.
2. Enhance the image of the Bishop through media and written publications as approved by the Bishop.
3. Oversee the development of an annual souvenir journal.

4. Maintain historical files of the activities of the Jurisdiction.

5. Coordinate the scheduling of special events in jurisdictional facilities.

6. Promote and market the use of jurisdictional facilities

7. Negotiate and get approved, contracts with vendors during jurisdictional activities

8. Procure, contract and schedule special events pending the approval of the jurisdictional Bishop.

Specific Responsibilities:

1. Solicit appropriate information concerning pending activities from each department and communicate those activities to the media.

2. Communicate the annual goals of each department to the public.

3. Obtain annual goals for the jurisdiction and communicate the activities associated with those goals to the jurisdiction and the general public.

4. Maintain professionalism through attending conventions, workshops, seminars, etc., keeping

abreast of latest developments in Christian and secular literature.

5. Give leadership to the development and maintenance of a jurisdictional website.

6. Work individually and cooperatively with the Bishop and his assistants in developing and implementing the Jurisdictional policies and goals in reference to public relations.

7. Obtain permission from the Bishop before releasing any information regarding the jurisdiction or national church that has been obtained from other sources.

8. Provide leadership in training other public relations workers in the Jurisdiction.

9. Provide copies of contracts with price disclosures and letters of confirmation to persons who contract to utilize jurisdictional facilities.

10. Contact approved personnel for contracted events I.e., janitorial services, security, sound and lighting personnel

GENERAL DUTIES

1. DPR implements a Jurisdiction wide plan for community relations and marketing to enhance the Jurisdiction's image and

presence.

2. DPR implements community relation's strategies that promote awareness of Jurisdictional empowerment efforts.

3. DPR pursues business and community resources and volunteers to support the efforts of the Jurisdiction and the Vision of the Bishop.

4. DPR creates and revises community outreach training and support materials.

5. DPR facilitates Jurisdictional special events and writes nominations for awards recognizing jurisdictional and community members.

6. DPR develops marketing materials for the Jurisdiction and local churches to be used in their community outreach efforts.

7. Conducts development functional programs that include assisting in strategic fundraising.

8. DPR collaborates with Jurisdictional District programs to assist with marketing and public relations and provide support as requested by the District Superintendent.

SPECIFIC DUTIES

- **Press including:**
- Liaison with local community press.
- Issue of press notes, bulletins and news release to the local community press.
- Provide for visit of local community press representatives to Jurisdictional functions in the different areas to promote the Jurisdictional Bishop's vision.
- Arrangement of press conference for Jurisdictional Bishop on issues of importance to the Church and the community.
- Publication and display of classified advertisements in newspapers release.
- Publication of publicity literature, i.e., pamphlet, poster, brochures, etc. in different languages regarding the achievements and developments Jurisdictional programs of the Jurisdictional Bishop.
  - Publicity of the achievements of the Jurisdiction and the Vision of the Jurisdictional Bishop within and outside the Jurisdictional of Oklahoma through available media programs.

Exhibition:
- To arrange exhibitions within and outside the Jurisdiction.
- Production of Jurisdictional newsletter, Souvenir Journal documentary and feature films and tape ministry.
- Liaison with All area radio-and television

stations.

- Publicity through television.
- Field publicity.
- Develop an Information Center or digital system for disseminating pertinent jurisdictional information and or notices

Community Outreach

- This includes communications and marketing strategies, to create a liaison and coordinator to reach the entire Jurisdiction Community by community.
- Facilitating partnership agreements with a yearlong plan to focus on getting the Jurisdictional Bishop's message throughout the entire Jurisdiction.
- Troubleshooting find those area that needs improvement, developing a program to accomplish this.
- Recruiting new partners to support jurisdictional functions
- Recognizing exemplary partners and partnership activities.
- Evaluating partnerships for relevance or effectiveness of continued collaboration.

Ministry Specific Goals:

- Focus on promoting and enhancing attendance at jurisdictional services
- Build a team of volunteers that will advance the mission of the jurisdiction through charitable

projects in conjunction with the Jurisdictional Department of Missions
- Give leadership and or support to the team involved in the jurisdictional website.

Education and Experience:
- Have a degree in journalism, public relations, advertising or other communications-related field
- Or this position may be held by one with life experiences or a student in the above mentioned fields of study

Special Skills:
- A strong command of the English Language, both written and spoken. Demonstrate creativity, initiative, good judgment, decision-making, research and problem solving skills.
- Proficiency with the latest word processing, desktop publishing, graphics and website maintenance applications.

JURISDICTIONAL POLITICAL ACTION COMMITTEE[7]

PURPOSE OF THE COMMITTEE

This is a jurisdictional appointment by the Bishop to activate the following:

- Conduct Voter Registration Campaign for the current elections

- Steering Committee to promote the absentee ballot initiative

  - Promote: Registration, Education and Mobilization

  - Recruit Volunteers

- Review and Promote Activities for Civic Engagement and Involvement.

---

[7] This is an optional Committee for the Jurisdiction

PHILOSOPHY

As a 501(c) (3) tax-exempt religious organization, the Church of God in Christ, Inc. is prohibited from participating in political campaigns on behalf of, or in opposition to, a candidate for public office. Therefore, the Church of God in Christ, Inc. (COGIC), including any individual acting on behalf of COGIC, will not engage in any of the following political activities: Donating Church of God in Christ funds to a candidate's campaign, participating or engaging in political fundraising events, publishing material for any candidate's campaign, participating or engaging in political fundraising events, publishing or distributing statements for or against any candidate, or engaging in any other activity that favors or opposes a political candidate.

Mission Statement

The Mission of the Political Action Committee of the Oklahoma Southeast Ecclesiastical Jurisdiction is to increase the awareness of Voter Registration. The Political Action Committee shall educate the Oklahoma Southeast Jurisdiction saints about why it is important to vote, as well as the results of not voting. The Political Action Committee shall be nonpartisan and shall not endorse candidates for public office.

Objectives

- The Political Action Committee shall seek to increase registration and voting.
- Keep the individuals of the Jurisdiction informed of all proposed legislation that affects minority groups.
- To integrate political awareness within Oklahoma Southeast Jurisdiction at the local level, and District level.
- To enrich and educate individuals of political current events that take place in the Jurisdictional as well as the U.S. (Local, Jurisdictional, and internationally).

Vision

The vision of the Political Action Committee is to recruit as many volunteers as possible to help to communicate the necessity and responsibility of voting. The "Souls to the Polls" Campaign will engage in locating all individuals 18 years of age and older to either register to vote for the very first time, or renew their registration. Voter Registration shall be a major issue tackled by not only the Jurisdiction but the African American population as well. Whatever revenues and or sources that need to be taken will be to assure that all saints are registered as well as to have a record high number of individuals registered in the Jurisdiction.

Sub- Committees

Preface: The following Sub-Committees will help the Political Action Committee in its decision-making and will make up the Committee itself. The sub-committees will keep the Chairman of the Committee updated on all happenings that will affect the Jurisdiction regarding voting. The following subcommittes are identified as follows:

Community Coordinator:

- Contact different areas to see if access is available for Jurisdictional Voter Registration setups.
- Keep the Chairman updated on Community happenings across the Jurisdictional (Political, School Boards, etc.)

Fundraising:

- Committee will devise different ideas that will help raise funds in order for the P.A.C. to function (especially with travel expense, food, etc.)
- Keep the Chairman and the Bishop updated on such projected ideas.

Public Relations:

- Will be responsible for creating such things as flyers, brochures, etc. to the Local, District, and Jurisdictional members.

ABSENTEE BALLOTT INITIATIVE

The mission of the Presiding Bishop Absentee Ballot Initiative is religious, not a targeted political strategy but simply an Episcopal Call to Political Responsibility supporting an electoral process for a just and sustainable world. The Church of God in Christ, Inc. does not endorse or challenge candidates for election to public office.

SOULS TO THE POLLS CAMPAIGN

1. FOCUS: Registration, Education and Mobilization

2. UNDERSTAND: Voting requirements for absentee balloting and guidelines

3. PREPARE: Prepare and train voting volunteers, map a schedule of activities

4. MEET: Encourage collaboration with local election board

5. Develop consciences and encourage all eligible voters to participate in the electoral process.

6. Nurture and support enthusiasm for absentee ballot voting

7. Educate churches and pastors on the importance of Biblically faithful voters to vote their Biblical values

8. Partner with pastors and churches to encourage members to participate in the election process.

STRATEGY FOR IMPLEMENTATION

1. Organize the Steering Committee

2. Recruit Representatives in each district

3. Recruit Volunteers to assist in all areas:

   a. Registration

   b. Information dissemination

   c. Transportation

   d. Announcements and fliers

   e. Booths for registration in each meeting prior to election

   f. Contact persons for city council and Jurisdictional legislature

   g. Communicate new voter information to jurisdiction

4. Contact by letter and schedule meeting with the Oklahoma County Election Chairman

5. Send letters to all counties in which we have churches

6. Solicit assistance of churches with vans to motor pool people to the polls

7. Set up registration and absentee material in each church through the districts

8. Keep informed about the national committee appointed by the Presiding Bishop

9. There is a regional coordinator for each area of jurisdictions

FLOW CHARTS FOR

FISCAL RESPONSIBILITY

Administrative Hierarchy

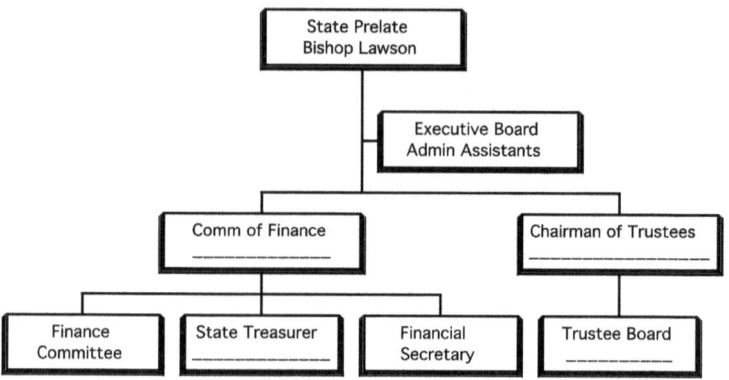

Procedures for Receiving and Depositing Funds

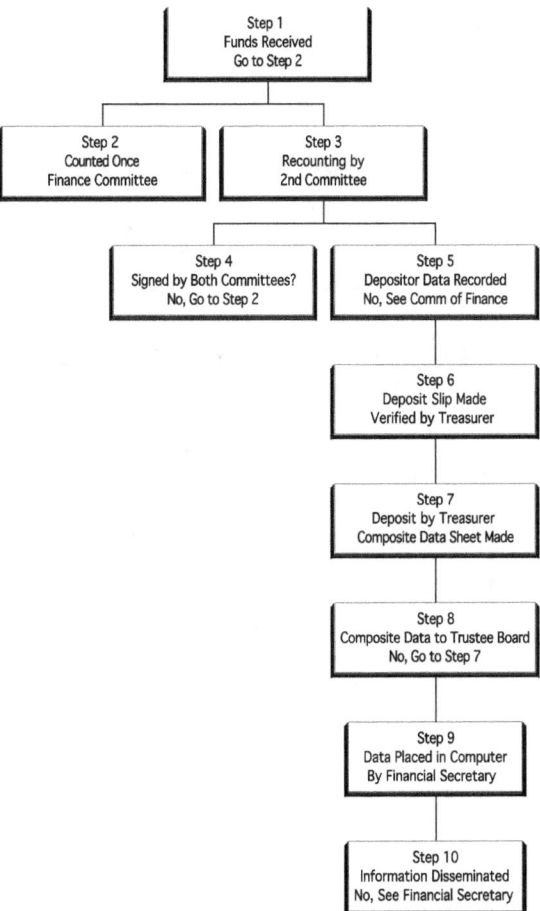

Step 1
Funds Received
Go to Step 2

Step 2
Counted Once
Finance Committee

Step 3
Recounting by
2nd Committee

Step 4
Signed by Both Committees?
No, Go to Step 2

Step 5
Depositor Data Recorded
No, See Comm of Finance

Step 6
Deposit Slip Made
Verified by Treasurer

Step 7
Deposit by Treasurer
Composite Data Sheet Made

Step 8
Composite Data to Trustee Board
No, Go to Step 7

Step 9
Data Placed in Computer
By Financial Secretary

Step 10
Information Disseminated
No, See Financial Secretary

PROCEDURES FOR RECEIVING FUNDS

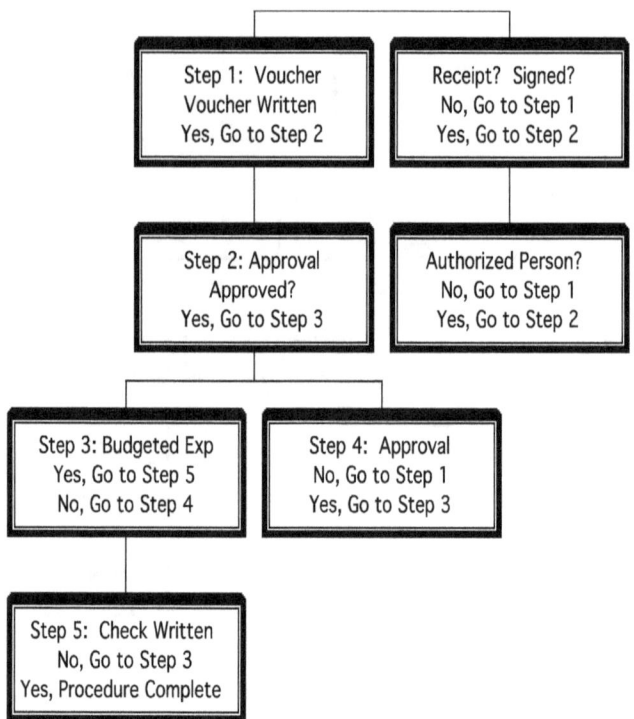

Step 1: Voucher
Voucher Written
Yes, Go to Step 2

Receipt? Signed?
No, Go to Step 1
Yes, Go to Step 2

Step 2: Approval
Approved?
Yes, Go to Step 3

Authorized Person?
No, Go to Step 1
Yes, Go to Step 2

Step 3: Budgeted Exp
Yes, Go to Step 5
No, Go to Step 4

Step 4: Approval
No, Go to Step 1
Yes, Go to Step 3

Step 5: Check Written
No, Go to Step 3
Yes, Procedure Complete

REFERENCES

Boyd, Thomas, Accounting *Systems for Churches,* Minneapolis: Augsburg Publishing House, 1984.

Coby, Malcolm W., *Handbook for Church Organization, Administration and Ministry,* Oklahoma City: Victory Publications, 2014.

Lindsey, Bishop D.L. *Church of God in Christ History, Theology and Structure,* Little Rock: Jurisdictional Press, 1990.

Perry, Enoch, *Church of God in Christ Sexual Misconduct Policy,* Church of God in Christ Publishing House, 2007.

Range, Elder C. F., editor, *Official Manual with the Doctrines and Discipline of the Church of God in Christ, Inc.,* Memphis: Church of God in Christ Publishing House, 1973.

Williams, Matthew, editor, *The National Adjutancy, Church of God in Christ 2014 Pocket Guide,* Memphis, Tennessee

www.ingramcontent.com/pod-product-compliance
Lightning Source LLC
Chambersburg PA
CBHW060628290526
45793CB00001B/190